Dear Reader:

You visited Peru, enjoyed the landscape, the people and of course, the food. Perhaps you have been a victim of the Atahualpa Revenge and pledged no come back again even when you are missing Peru already.

Perhaps you left Peru some time ago and would like to cook your food with the ingredients you can find in your new country of residence.

Perhaps you are a collector of tastes and sensations and would enjoy reproducing our wonderful food.

Living outside Peru for more than ten years has been a great challenge. However, no one time have I been left without the ingredients for a good amount of recipes.

Today we want to present you with some basic recipes from the Peruvian Cooking hoping you will find them useful. Peruvian dishes are full of natural flavour taken from the vegetables and meats, not from the condiments and that explains the simplicity and taste. We wish you a good start.

Contents:

Starters.

Chilli Sauce 6
1. Huancayo Style Potato. 7
2. Marinated Fish 9
3. Mussels Callao Style 11
4. Russian Eggs 13
5. Russian Salad 14
6. Stuffed Avocado 15

Soups.

1. Butternut Squash Cream 17
2. Chicken Soup 18
3. Beef Stew 19

Main Courses.

Peruvian White Rice 21
1. Cabbage Stew 22
2. Covered Rice 23
3. Dry Beef Stew 25
4. Quinoa with Milk 27
5. Turmeric Chicken 29
6. White Beans 31

Desserts.

Mange Blanc 34
1. Rice Pudding 35
2. Stuffed Figs 36
3. Wedding biscuits 37

STARTERS

chilli sauce

(S A L S A D E A J I)

Peruvian Food is often served with chilli sauce. The preparation is different in every home. Try this very simple sauce:

Ingredients:

* 250 gm. Fresh chilli
* 1 clove of garlic
* salt and water.

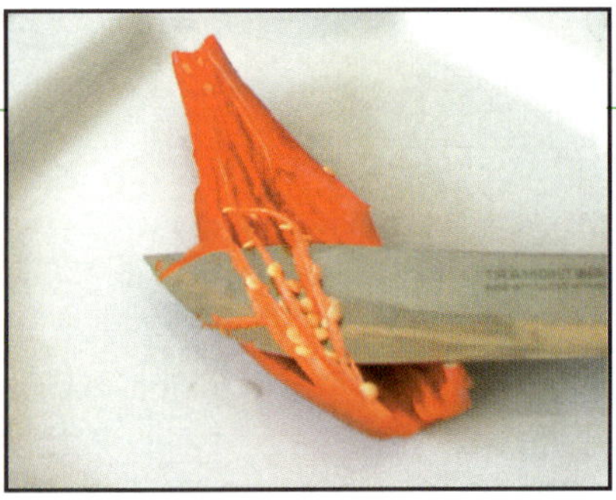

Preparation:

* Wash and open the chilli, removing the tips.
* Open the chillies lengthways and using a knife or a teaspoon remove vein and seeds.
* Put the chilli, garlic, salt and 50 ml of water in a blender and blend for about 2 min, or until the chilli and garlic have become a paste.
* Serve in a bowl.

huancayo style potato

(PAPA A LA HUANCAINA)

The Huancayo style potato is prepared differently in every home. You will find cooked and uncooked sauces, all of which are delicious. This is my motherí s recipe.

Ingredients (serves 4):

* 3 medium size potatoes.
* 250 gm. Ricotta, Mascarpone or Feta cheese.
* 1 or 2 fresh chillies (or fresh chilli sauce).
* 1 lime or l/2 lemon.
* 2 tablespoons of vegetable oil.
* 100 ml water.
* salt.
* 1 fresh corn on the cob.
* 2 hard-boiled eggs.

Preparation:

* Cook the potatoes in a cooking pan with water and a pinch of salt for about 30 min.
* When they are ready (a fork will go through them easily) let them cool and then peel.
* Cook the sweetcorn in thick slices.
* To prepare the sauce, mix all the ingredients in a bowl adding the water at the end. If you have fresh chilli or Feta cheese, blend with water. The sauce should have a medium thick consistency. Add more water if necessary.
* The colour of the sauce will vary depending on the colour of the chilli.

* To serve it, dress a plate with some lettuce leaves, slice the potato and serve on top of the lettuce. Cover the potato with the sauce and garnish with an olive, hard-boiled egg or slice of sweetcorn.

marinated fish

(S E B I C H E)

This particular dish is found along the whole South American Pacific Coast. Every Country prepares and presents it differently. The common point is the way the fish or seafood is cooked: by marinating it in lemon juice, lime juice or vinegar with spices and chilli. The taste varies depending on the kind of fish you use. This version is my own recipe. (I come from Lima, Capital City of Peru) and this version reflects the Limenian Cooking. I hope you enjoy it.

Ingredients (serves 4):

* 500 gm of white fish fillet (Plaice) chopped into 2cm square pieces.
* 7 limes.
* 1 small red onion. (If necessary, a white onion sliced quite thickly will do).
* 1 or 2 fresh chillies.
* salt and pepper.
* 1 fresh corn on the cob, cooked in slices.
* If you cannot get corn on the corn, use canned sweetcorn.
* 1 large sweet potato, boiled and peeled.
* 2 celery sticks, sliced very thinly.
* 1 tablespoon of parsley (flat or curly), finely chopped.
* Some lettuce leaves to garnish the dish.

Preparation:

* Put the fish together with the onion, celery and chilli in a bowl.
* Add the lemon or lime juice and season with salt and pepper.
* Mix carefully and cover for about 20 min.

Once the fish is cooked (you will notice that it is not translucent any more and that the texture is different than before), put it in the fridge to stop it cooking further. Taste it and add salt, pepper or chilli if required.
Serve the sebiche with thick slices of the sweet potato, slices of the sweetcorn (about 1 inch thick) and serve on a bed of lettuce.

mussels callao style

(CHOROS A LA CHALACA)

It is possible to find packed mussels in the supermarkets imported from Europe, South America or Oceania, the last ones being more similar in taste to Peruvian mussels, which is no surprise as they come from the same ocean! You can also find mussels in the markets. This is a very nice recipe.

Ingredients (serves 4):

* 1 1/2 dozen fresh, clean mussels.
* 1 medium size onion, chopped finely.
* 1 chilli, veined, seeded and chopped very finely.
* The juice of 1 lime or lemon.
* The cooked kernels of 1 corn on the cob.
* 1 tablespoon of parsley leaves, finely chopped.
* salt and pepper.
* 3 tablespoons of vegetable oil.

Preparation:

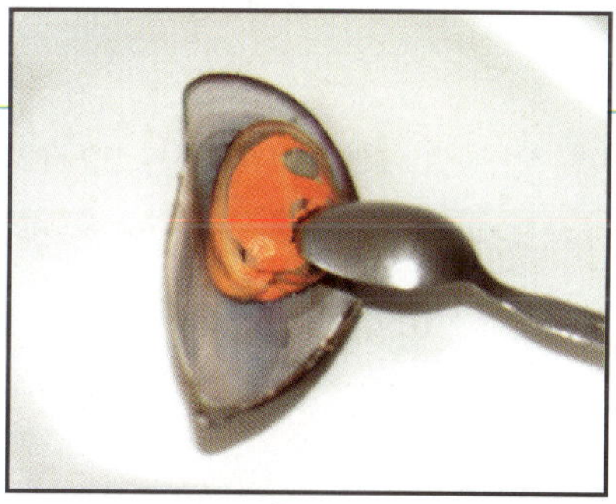

If you buy fresh mussels:

* Boil the mussels in enough water to cover them until they open. Discard any that do not open.
* Remove one half of the shell.

If you buy packed open ones:

* Allow them to boil for 1 or 2 min and let them cool.
* Clean every one, removing the digestive tract.

* Mix the onion, sweetcorn kernels, chilli and parsley in a bowl. Add the lime or lemon juice, salt, pepper and vegetable oil. Allow it to infuse.
* Taste and add salt or pepper if necessary to your taste.
* Once the mixture has infused for about 15 min pour it on top of every mussel .
* This dish can be served as finger food, or in individual portions, as below.

* Another way to serve it is to remove the mussels totally from their shells and prepare a salad with all the ingredients.

russian eggs

(H U E V O S A L A R U S A)

Ingredients (serves 4):

* 2 hard-boiled eggs.
* 200 gm. Russian Salad.
* 1 cup of mayonnaise.
* Lettuce leaves.
* 3 or 4 tablespoons of tomato Ketchup.
* Parsley leaves to garnish.

Preparation:

Pink Sauce:

* Add the tomato sauce to the mayonnaise stirring slowly until it becomes pink. It is better to start with half the amount in order to mix it to the consistency and flavour you desire.
* Garnish a plate with lettuce.
* Add 2 generous tablespoons of Russian Salad.
* Cut the eggs in half and add on top.
* Cover with the pink sauce.

russian salad

(E N S A L A D A R U S A)

In Peru we eat Russian Salad as a starter. It serves also as a basic ingredient for other dishes such as Stuffed Avocado or Russian Eggs.

Ingredients (serves 6):

* 100 gm. of fresh peas.
* 100 gm. of fresh French beans or fine beans.
* 2 medium sized carrots, finely chopped.
* 2 cooked medium sized potatoes, peeled and and finely chopped.
* The kernels of 1 corn on the cob.
* 1 cup of fresh mayonnaise.
* Salt. * Lettuce leaves.

Preparation:

* Even though some Chefs recommend cooking the ingredients separately, we cook them together, except for the potato. It is better to boil it with the skin on and peel it when cooked. Add salt.
* When everything is cooked properly (do not let it to over cook), remove, sieve and allow to cool down.
* Transfer the cold vegetables to a bowl, adding the finely chopped potato.
* Stir it until the mayonnaise covers all the ingredients.

To serve, garnish a plate with the lettuce leaves, serve the salad using a mould and finish with an olive, feta cheese, hard-boiled egg or whatever you wish.

stuffed avocado

(P A L T A   R E L L E N A)

This is a very traditional Peruvian dish, which I hope you enjoy.

Ingredients (serves 2):

* 1 Ripe avocado.
* 200 gm Russian Salad.
* Lettuce leaves.
* Salt.

Preparation:

* Garnish a plate with lettuce leaves.
* Open the avocado and remove the stone.
* Slice the bottom. Place on the lettuce.
* Add salt and 2 tablespoons of salad.
* Add some mayonnaise on top.

SOUPS

butternut squash cream

(C R E M A   D E   Z A P A L L O)

All the pumpkins and squashes have slightly different flavours. I am very keen in the butternut squash (small pear like with a nutty taste). However, you only need to find one that suits your appetite for flavour.

Ingredients (serves 4):

* 1 Butternut squash cut and peeled (cutting it first will protect you from cutting yourself).
* 1 can of evaporated milk, 250 ml fresh cream or 250 ml full fat milk (any of them will do).
* 1 tablespoon butter.
* Salt. * Water.
* A small piece of Feta cheese or hard-boiled egg (squashed with a fork) to garnish.

Preparation:

* Boil the squash until it separates (10 min approximately) with 200ml water.
* Once cooked blend it with the water.
* Return it to the pan and add some milk.
* Add salt and butter and boil it for 1 min.
* Turn the heat off, serve and garnish.

chicken soup

(SOPA DE POLLO)

Peruvian chicken soup is prepared by boiling the chicken with the other ingredients. It is very tasty and has a concentrated flavour, depending on which part of chicken you use. For soup I prefer to use legs. However, any part will give you very good flavour.

Ingredients (serves 4):

* Four chicken legs without the skin
* 2 large carrots cut in half.
* 1 small stick of celery.
* 1 medium sized leek, sliced.
* Salt.
* Noodles (optional).

Preparation:

* Boil all the ingredients with enough water to cover them.
* Allow the ingredients to boil in high heat for about 10 min, then reduce the heat to medium until the carrots are cooked or for about half an hour.

Sieve the soup adding noodles if using them.

Serve the soup with a chicken piece, carrot and some celery if serving as the main course.

beef stew

(SANCOCHADO)

This stew clearly reflects the Spanish influence on Peru. The taste comes from cooking the different ingredients together. There are restaurants in Peru famous for their ìFriday Beef Stewî. I hope you like it.

Ingredients (serves 4):

* 500 gm. Rib, Rib eye or Brisket (If you can get it on the bone, the weight will be more than that, probably 1 kg).
* 2 corn on the cob, cut in half.
* 1 small Savoy cabbage, cut in half.
* 1 large stick of Celery, clean without leaves.
* 4 medium size potatoes, peeled.
* 4 large carrots, peeled.
* 1 yam or cassava, peeled.
* 2 large sweet potatoes or 4 small ones, peeled. * Salt.

Preparation:

* Boil the beef for I hour.
* After the first 10 min add the carrots, sweetcorn and the greens. Season.
* Add the remaining ingredients in this order: Potatoes, yam, and lastly sweet potato.

You can start with all the ingredients together, but will need to remove ingredients from the pan once cooked.

* Serve the solids on a plate and the soup, on a soup bowl. Accompany with chilli sauce.

MAIN COURSES

Peruvian white rice

(A R R O Z B L A N C O)

Peru has an extraordinary history of immigration through the last 5 centuries. Each group of people who came to Peru brought their culinary traditions with them. The Chinese migrants from the 19th century brought rice with them. Rice is eaten almost every day, sometimes twice a day. The way we cook it has a Spanish influence.

Ingredients (serves 4):

* 1 garlic clove sliced, chopped or squashed.
* 3 tablespoons of vegetable oil.
* 1 teaspoon of salt.
* 2 cups of long grain rice.
* 2 cups water.

Preparation:

* Wash the rice carefully avoiding spilling it until the water runs almost clear.
* In a medium size pan fry the garlic until golden (no more than a minute).
* Add the water, the rice and the salt. Stir.
* Allow to boil stirring 2 or 3 times until it dries.
* When the water dries out add 1 tablespoon of vegetable oil, stir again and cover with a lid. Reduce the heat to medium.
* Wait for about 10minutes and remove from the hob. Stir it once more.

cabbage stew

(GUISO DE REPOLLO)

For as long as I can remember I have eaten this stew. My mother used to cook it and I loved it. She used tiny pieces of beef (we did not have mince then). Today I use mince and my grandson, who is 2 years old, really likes it. I hope you will too.

Ingredients (serves 6):

* 500 gm good minced beef (as lean as possible).
* 1 small cabbage chopped into strips.
* 1 medium sized tomato, chopped.
* 4 medium size potatoes, chopped into quarters.
* Salt.
* 3 tablespoons of vegetable oil.

Preparation:

* Fry the mince until cooked.
* Add the tomato, cook for 5 min.
* Add 1/2 l water, then salt.
* Add the potatoes and the cabbage. Cover with a lid. Stir at least twice to make the cabbage go down inside the pan.
* Cook on a medium heat for 20 min or until the potato is cooked.

  Serve with rice and chilli sauce.

covered rice

(ARROZ TAPADO)

Ingredients (serves 4):

* 250 gm of lean minced beef.
* 100 gm raisins or sultanas, finely sliced.
* 100 gm kalamata olives (Greek style), pitted and sliced.
* 1 medium size onion, finely chopped.
* 2 hard-boiled eggs, chopped in squares.
* 3 tablespoons of vegetable oil.
* Salt.

Preparation:

* In a frying pan heat the oil at high temperature.
* Fry the meat until it changes colour (5 min).
* Add the onion, stir it allowing it to cook.
* When the onion is cooked, add the sultanas, olives and water. Boil for 5 min on a medium heat. Add salt after tasting the mix.
* When cooked turn off the heat.

  Add the hard-boiled egg.

  This mix can now be used to prepare delicious dishes like stuffed potatoes, potato pie, etc.

This is one way of serving covered rice:

* Fill one third of a cooking mould or cup with fresh made white rice.
* Fill the next third of the mould or cup with the mince mixture.
* Cover the rest with rice.
* Serve with a garnish of lettuce leaves and tomato. It should be turned out of the mould or cup with a swift movement.

dry beef stew

(SECO DE CARNE)

You will find this stew in every in every North Peruvian Restaurant along with the beans.

Ingredients (serves 6):

* 500 gm stewing beef cut in 3 to 4 cm pieces. (If using ribs buy 1kg)
* 1 kg. Yam or Cassava, peeled and cut in 10 cm. Pieces.
* 1 large onion diced.
* 2 good sized bunches of coriander leaves.
* 4 tablespoons of vegetable oil.
* Salt.
* 200 gm of fresh peas.

Preparation:

* Heat the oil and fry the beef.
* Add the onion when all the beef is sealed (every side fried until brown) and stir to cook it evenly.
* Blend the coriander leaves with water.
* When the onion is caramelised add the coriander and salt.
* Add enough water to cover the ingredients by 2cm.
* Cover .
* Cook at 200C for 15 min. Add the yam and peas and cook for about 40 min if using ribs or 30 min. if using stewing beef.

* Keep checking the water making sure there is a good amount of it.
* When the yam is soft and the beef is done, remove from the heat. Serve it with rice.

You may also serve as part of a large dish as illustrated below.

quinoa with milk

(QUINUA CON LECHE)

You should find quinoa in most health foods stores, which is a testatement to its goodness.

Ingredients (serves 4):

* 250 gm. of quinoa.
* 250gm. of white potatoes cut in quarters.
* 2 tablespoons of vegetable oil.
* 250 ml of milk (fresh or tinned)
* 125 gm. of fresh cheese (feta or ricotta).
* 1 teaspoon of chilli sauce.
* Salt.

Preparation:

* Wash the quinoa in very gently adding water slowly and calmly. Change the water 3 to 4 times. Discard any floating grains.
* Put the quinoa and potatoes in a pan and add water. The water should cover the quinoa and potatoes by at least 2cm.
* Boil for about 20 min or until the potato is ready. (The quinoa will have changed size and colour).
* If it becomes too dry add a little more of water.
* Once cooked add oil, salt, milk and chilli sauce. Stir and leave to cook for 2 more min at low heat.
* Crumble the feta cheese and add. If you are using ricotta add it without crumbling.

Serve it with rice, meat or fried egg. As it is very rich in proteins I just serve it with rice.

turmeric chicken

(CAU CAU DE POLLO)

Usually, the main ingredient for cau cau is tripe.. However, as this is difficult to find instead I prepare cau cau with chicken, which give us a very tasty result. I hope you like it.

Ingredients (serves 4):

* 500 gm of chicken breasts skinned and boned.
* 1 medium sized onion chopped finely.
* 500 gr. of white potatoes chopped in squares about 2cm in size.
* 1 tablespoon of turmeric powder.
* chilli sauce (optional)
* 3 tablespoon of parsley leaves fine chopped.
* 4 tablespoon of vegetable oil
* Salt
* 200 gm. fresh peas.
* 750ml water.

Preparation:

* Heat 2 tablespoon of oil. Donít allow it to smoke.
* Fry the chicken until cooked. (about 5 min)
  Stir then remove from the hob.
* In another frying pan fry the onion with the rest of the oil.
* When it changes colour add the Turmeric salt and chilli.
* Put the chicken back on the hob.
* Add all the rest of ingredients starting with the onion. Do not forget to season.

* Boil the potato until cooked.
  (About 15 min on a medium heat).
* Do not allow the potato to over boil.
- Taste and add more salt if necessary.
  Simply serve the Cau cau with rice and maybe
  Baked sweet potato.

white beans

(FREJOLES BLANCOS)

In Peru, as in all South and Central America, beans are eaten as part of the staple diet. Depending on the region whitebeans will come as part of a main course. In itself white beans are both nutritious and cheap

Ingredients (serves 4):

* 250 gm. of haricot beans.
* 1 small piece of pork skin (50 gm)
* 1 small sized onion chopped fine.
* 1 medium sized tomato chopped.
* Salt
* 3 tablespoons of vegetable oil

Preparation:

* Wash and soak the beans for at least 8 hours in plenty of water until they swell.
* Cook the beans in a pan for at least one hour, on high heat the first 20min, then medium the Resting time. Do not allow the water to evaporate. If needed add boiling water.

* While the beans boil fry the onion, adding the tomato when the onion is cooked.
* When the tomato is cooked, add to the Beans. Add the pork skin and boil for 30 min.

* When the beans are cooked (they are Soft) add the salt, and keep cooking for 15 min.

* Remove the pork skin.

* Serve with rice.

DESSERTS

mange blanc

(MANJAR BLANCO)

This sweet is one of the oldest in Peru. It was prepared during the Spanish Colony in the 16th century. The Incas did not know of Sugar, therefore the idea of eating something sugary but fruit after meals is obviously Spanish. Its use is extended to all South America. This recipe is a cheat as it involves a pre prepared ingredient.

Ingredients:

* 1 Can of Condensed milk.

Preparation:

* In a Pressure Cooker cover the can with water. Close the lid and boil it for 2 hours. Follow the Pressure Cooker Instructions regarding boiling for a long time.
* Remove the can and wait until it is totally cold before opening.
* Use as an ingredient for other desserts or as a dessert in itself.

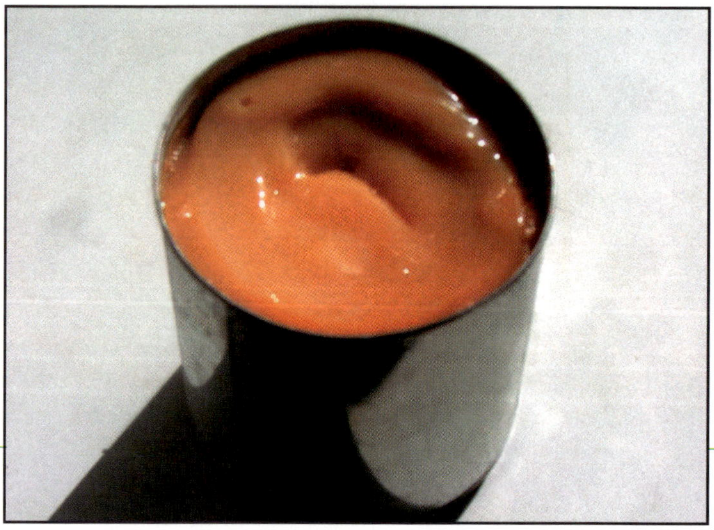

rice pudding

(ARROZ CON LECHE)

Even though you find Rice Pudding everywhere, ours has its own flavour. Try this. recipe

Ingredients:

* 250 gm of rice.
* 150 gm of sugar.
* 1 cinnamon stick.
* 1 teaspoon of vanilla essence.
* 1 tin of evaporated.
* Cinnamon powder.

Preparation:

* Wash the rice.
* Cook the rice with two cups of water the vanilla and the cinnamon until The rice is cook.
* Add the milk and sugar, Boil for 1 min on medium heat
* Remove from the hob.
* Serve in a bowl, adding cinnamon Powder on top.

stuffed figs

(HIGOS RELLENOS)

Ingredients:

* 250 gm of dry figs.
* 100 gm of Mange Blanc.
* 50 gm.of sugar.
* 1 tablespoon of Hundreds and Thousands.
* 1 cup of water.

Preparation:

* Boil the figs and sugar with the cup of water For (15 min).
* Wait until the water becomes syrup.
* Remove from the hob.
* When the figs are cold, open them with a knife.
* Fill the figs with Mange Blanc.
* Sprinkle with Hundreds and Thousands.